Chapter 1

Introduction

Now lets take up or questions one by one and try to answer them making the concepts as simple as possible for all of you to understand and use in the corresponding field.

Now before jumping right into the definition of what are wormholes we must first understand what are white hole and black holes, this is because if we easily understand these structures then it will be a lot easier to understand the main topic of this book.

Black holes can be defined as stars collapsed under their own gravity which end up deforming and warping the light fabric of space and time. These are regions in the space defined with their immense gravity so enormous that even light cannot escape through it. Now this was a basic definition of black holes, moving to our definition on white holes we get a similar but opposite definition. The white holes can be defined as warps in the region of space time which will expel the material out of their horizons. If the black holes are known to such things up the white holes on the contrary are known to release things out.

Now the reason behind describing these two things was that the wormholes are a composition of both these holes. Means if we join the black hole and the white holes neck to neck what we get is a now structure in the region of space which shows up two properties at both of its ends, one end consists of a black hole which engulfs the matter in vicinity and the other is the white hole which expels things out leading to a creation of a path.

Now in simple terms a wormhole is a short path in the space which connects two distant regions of space thus reducing the distance between them.

Now a question may arise in the mind of the readers on why are these termed as wormholes?

If you all are thinking that does the name of these structures have any kind of relation with worms, then the answer is a wide yes. Let me show you how

For the illustration of wormholes in a simple way when it was an initial concept, the scientists used a very creative way to describe it and named the structures on the definition created then.

The illustration involved a simple experiment in real life. Consider a situation where we have a simple apple and a worm sitting on it trying to eat it, sorry for the fate of the worm it spots a sparrow which is about to make the worm it's pray. Now to avoid this, worm decides to move to the other side of apple where it can easily hide from the sparrow. To do this the worm has two ways either to go all around the apple or to simple consume

Man Made wormholes: An unsolved mystery

This book is a continuation to the first book in the series published already that is the 'Bhvansh Theory of Black holes'. These series of books that are being published mainly concentrates on the basics of space and black holes and tries to answer some of the mysterious questions in the history of astrophysics with the help of some formulas discovered by the author in the past 6 years.

In the book published earlier the author tried to press over the question of can we move through different black holes and provided a simple mathematical formula which will give an output in the form of different velocities for the input of different mass of the black holes that the user wants to interact with.

Now in this particular book the author decides to concentrate on the theorem of man-made wormholes or also known as the transversable wormholes. The main part of the book written describes what are the transversable wormholes? Are there are any practical proofs which make the existence of these wormholes evident. Is each wormhole transversable? How can the wormholes be formed?

The answers to all these questions will be given in a chronological order, but first we will start with a basic introduction which will form the basis for our first chapter.

Table of contents

the apple to make a small tunnel through end and reach the other end as quickly as possible. Supposing our worm is smart enough and opts for the second way and in this procedure the tunnel created can be termed as a wormhole.

The thing which the wormhole did for the worm in the case of the apple is same to what the wormholes in the region of space do. The only difference between them is that one is made in case of an apple and the other is made in the region of space.

Now there are two major kinds of wormholes:

1.) The transversable wormholes: The are the wormholes through which the humans can easily pass through and these can be used as our teleportation devices to the other universes
2.) The non transversable wormholes: These are the wormholes through which the humanity cant travel and for the description of these wormholes a new theorem of singularity will be included in the subsequent chapters of the books.

Although the presence of the wormholes remained a question in the field of astrophysics for a very long time but the question was answered recently by a group of researchers at the California institute of Technology at USA by creating small baby wormhole on the Earth, the creation of such a wormhole was an open evidence that if the black holes can be created on Earth then they may even exist in the vast regions of the space, now the scientists are trying to study this wormhole in order to get the correct picture of the way they may exist actually.

Now with the setting of these basic things in our minds regarding the wormholes lets move onto the main formula discovered regarding the wormholes, it advantages, its obstacles and answering other main questions that have been put forward before.

Chapter 2:

The Main formula

Speaking of astrophysics it is a dynamic field, it is really correct to state it to be dynamic in nature as each passing day new theories are emerging trying to explain the phenomena that are occurring in the outer space, a similar attempt has been used by the author where he is trying to put forward a formula mathematically derived which will help us to calculate the mass of the matter needed to make a wormhole. The formula discovered has been presented below:

Note: The formula presented has been encoded and the exact meaning of symbols has not been presented but the formula if brought in front scientifically will help in knowing the exact thing that has been described above.

$$\text{Mass needed} = AP/DB$$

Here in the formula:

1.) A stands for something which is proportional to the mass of the black hole that we want to create in the form of a wormhole
2.) P stands for something that is proportional to the mass of the constituent Black hole needed to form a wormhole
3.) D stands for something that acts as an object which is inversely propotional to the mass of the wormhole which we want to create, it is something which is felt when somebody enters in the vicinity of the black hole, it depend on the mass of the shuttle that we are sending through the resulting black hole.
4.) B stands for the Black hole constant that will be used in the formula and will have the form of $1/t^2$ or the dimensionality will be $[M^oL^0T^{-2}]$ and will have the standard units of the form S^{-2} where S stands for seconds. This constant is of a great need as this will help in proving the dimensionality of the formula to be correct.

So above is the main formula that has been discovered and is really important as it will help us to know a lot about the black holes and the wormholes to such an extent that the overall knowledge of the humans will increase both holistically and on a wider scale. Now with the provision of the main formula lets move on to the next major part of this chapter which are the advantages and the disadvantages of this formula and what its use in the field of cosmos is.

Lets first start with the obstacles, and then we will take up their solutions and move up to the advantages.

Now let's consider some of the obstacles of the given formula:

1.) How to gather such a large mass: As form the given expression of the formula, it is quite clear and obvious at the first site that a huge amount of mass will be needed in order to create the black hole but how to gather such high mass. If we consider carrying such high mass with us it will be very difficult so the option that is left is to gather the mass from the universe that we have entered. Now it's a big problem as we don't know where the white hole will end. Till now it is quite probabilistic due to the presence of the maze wormhole. It is possible that we end up in such a region of the new universe where the resources are not available and if available they are very far off from our place of entry so in that case it makes gathering of matter quite impossible and this thing is one of the major drawback of the formula
2.) The wormhole may open into our original universe but we won't be able to find the path

back home : This drawback is quite possible, as discussed above a black hole is connected with various white holes at the same time, it is possible that when we make up the black hole it connects with a number of other white holes present nearby too along with the one white hole that we need in such a scenario what will happen is that the confusion of the maze wormhole will come up in our path and we won't be able to configure out that which wormhole will lead to our universe back.

3.) The process of formation may go wrong: As we know that to create a man made wormhole we have to concentrate the needed mass in small area so that the force is not well distributed but concentrated at a particular point as a result of which the space time tears apart. But there is a probability that while following the process it may go wrong and the whole concentrated matter gets converted into energy and explodes out, the explosion would be so large that it may destroy the main shuttle and may also kill the human life in it.

So above are the major obstacles in the formula, in order to resolve them we have to in particular perform a lot of experiments to come up with a new formula which provides us with the exact probability on how to successfully use the maze wormholes and find our path in it.

As we can see the obstacles are quite indeed very convincing and they may pose a great difficulty in the application of the formula.

As far as the solutions are concerned they will be discussed later in the coming chapter because before providing the solutions some more things have to be made clear so that when the solutions are presented they are understood properly and worked upon by all of you.

So now our next aim is to start working upon the advantages of the formula which will act as a motivation on why we should work upon this part of the research.

The advantages of the formula are:

1.) Helps to create wormholes: This formula is significant in itself as this formula allows us to create any kind of wormhole we want to create, and once we're able to create any kind of wormhole we aspire then we will not only be able to reach to distant places in the space but will also get an infinite source of energy in the form of black holes.

2.) Source of infinite amount of energy: Some of you might have thought that in the above advantage why have I used that infinite energy will be available to us in the form of black holes.

> The reason is quite simple, if we refer back to the basic definition of the wormholes we can relate that the wormholes are made up of black holes and white holes, and we also know that the black holes release gamma ray jets from their horizons, so if we are able to make the wormholes and are able to use them then we will also be able to use the black holes and under the use of proper technology we may be able to harness the excess energy the black holes provide then there will no longer exists the problem of energy levels on the Earth and to the human civilization.

So therefore it is quite evident that the formula is really helpful.

Now with the discussion of the advantages and the obstacles of the formula we will conclude with this chapter. And now it's the time to move to the next chapter. The next chapter will be indeed important as it will provide us with the ways on how different kind of wormholes are formed or especially how do the black holes combine in different forms. And after this chapter we will be well equipped to get the solutions of the obstacles labeled above.

Chapter 3

How do the black holes combine to form different structures

In this chapter I will present the main ways on how do the black holes combine to form different combinations and structures like wormholes.

I would like to discuss some of the laws that will help us find the black hole combinations and will conform how the black holes will form their respective combinations with white holes and will also conform with the information regarding which mass black hole will form a combination with which mass black hole:

Law 1) As a reference we will consider the Super massive black hole residing at the center of our galaxy, Sagittarius A as an ideal case and will formulate all the other laws regarding other black holes with reference to it in the home galaxy milky way.

Relevance of choosing Sagittarius A as an ideal case is because it is the nearest super massive black hole to the Earth present in our home galaxy Milky Way. Now because it is present very near to us it will be very easy to study and understand. So if we set it as an ideal case then it would be easy to formulate other laws effectively.

Law 2) the place where older singularities were considered to exist will be center of the total pathway between the black hole and its partner white hole.

The relevance of making such an assumption lies in the point that the radius of black holes was measured from the singularities of the black holes. The radius of any black hole was the distance in between the black hole and its corresponding singularity. But now when we have already mentioned and explained above that the singularities don't exist in super massive black hole but the space time is extended to form a white hole, the place where the singularity existed will act as a center along the path way, as from the center point only the graph started to move at an outer side and ended up forming a white hole. Thus it will be better and effective if we consider the singularity point as the center of the wormhole structure that will be formed. This law is really important as after this the main combinational laws will get started to form up. The point that must be considered here is that all the midpoint law as described is only applicable to the super massive black hole.

Law 3) According to specific galaxies a maximum limit will be set that to which point the space time graph can be penetrated. Now different galaxies are categorized on the basis of the super massive black hole which rests at their centers. The bigger the black hole at the center the bigger the galaxy. So therefore we can say the super massive black holes as a barometer in deciding the size of the home galaxy they reside in.

Not for this peculiar law it is very important to discuss that we are making such a weird assumption. This law is in full contradiction with the law that described to use Sagittarius A as a reference. Now the point here is that this law is the main law and the Law 1 can be considered as a sub type of this law. Basically this Is the only law according to which we formulated that we will choose Sagittarius A for reference but there it has been labeled that the reference of the Sagittarius A will be used only for the black holes present in that galaxy where that black hole resides that is the Milky way. Here in this law we are considering the different black holes in the different galaxies to be different types of writing pens and the space is considered to be a uniformly used paper. As different pens put different forces on the paper to tear it apart, the same is the case with different kind of black holes (super massive black holes). The different black holes exert a different force on the space, so we can't measure any black holes in reference to the other black hole. But the black holes within the same galaxy can be compared with reference to each other. So thus each and every galaxy will have a specific limit or a maximum limit to which the space can be penetrated and this limit will be decided on the basis of the most massive black hole present in that galaxy, usually the most massive black hole in any galaxy is the black hole residing at the center. So the limit that will be set will be in accordance to that black hole and at maximum that will be the only radius which will take hold of the longest distance between that black hole and its constituent partner the white hole. Thus the maximum a region can be ruptured corresponds to the radius of the most massive black hole that resides in that region. The region corresponds to a galaxy in the universe. This means that the other massive black holes would have the radius smaller than the radius of the largest black hole and this would also mean that the length of the longest wormhole tunnel that can be formed in the galaxy will correspond to the radius of the largest black hole and the other tunnel that might form will not be larger than that. Although this law may seem to be a little bit tricky at this point, but the law will be clear with the next two laws that I am going to mention.

Law 4) Now as we considered the singularity point to be the midpoint in case of the super massive black holes it is worth to note that the distance of the black hole and its partner white hole will be same from the midpoint and will be equal to the radius of the black hole as it has been calculated. This means that the length of the wormhole tunnel that will be formed corresponding to the black hole will be equal to two times the radius of the black hole. For example if we consider the case of the nearest super massive black hole Sagittarius A the tunnel it will likely form with the white hole will be equal to two times its present radius. The calculated radius of the Sagittarius-A black hole is around 22 million kilometers. So according to the Law 4, the length of its wormhole tunnel will correspond around 44 million Kilometers. Now any other black hole won't have such a long tunnel in the Milky Way till the time it is having a radius greater than the Sagittarius A. All the other massive black holes will have the length of the wormhole tunnel smaller than 44 million km, thus making the 44 million km a limit up to which the space in the Milky Way can be ruptured. This limit will remain intact until out of nowhere some other bigger black hole may enter the Milky Way galaxy. This law is very important is case of understanding how long we might have to travel if we want to travel through the Sagittarius A and further this law will indicate the time period it might take to cover the distance and for how long the shuttle will be exposed to the high gravitational force of the black hole. If somehow the exposure goes along for a long time then it will be advisable for us to not try to go through that particular black hole. So this law is very advantageous to us in point of view of the black hole travel. Now the next law will give us a fair explanation that why we took up to follow these two laws. The next law will somewhat will be a mixture of Law 3 that places the maximum limit that up to where the space time can be ruptured and law 4 which help us to find and discover the length of any wormhole that will be associated with any kind of super massive black holes. So we have to use these three formulas very effectively as they will help us to understand the black holes more clearly and effectively.

Law 5) This law explains that as explained if two black holes may interact with each other and may combine to form a singularity as explained many times above then the sum of the radius of the two black holes that will be connecting to form a singularity will be equal to the longest length of the wormhole that will be formed in a particular galaxy.

Now I want to create a link and make all of you understand these three laws that I have written, these are Law 3, Law 4 and most importantly Law 5. The combination of all these laws may appear to be a little tricky right now but once we will understand this relation between all the three laws then we will surely confirm that all my theories regarding the black hole formulations stated till now were true and those theories will one day help the humanity to better understand the concept of black holes more deeper than ever before. Now let's start maintaining a link between all these three laws and try to understand the concepts which are very necessary to study the black holes.

First of all as we have stated that the sum of the radius of the two black holes connecting will be equal to the length of the longest wormhole that may be formed in a particular galaxy. How will we know that what will be the length of the longest wormhole in a particular galaxy. For that we must know the largest black hole in that galaxy and from that we will know that it will rupture the space time in that region the most. Once we are clear with that part we would then calculate the radius of that black hole. Once we are through with this information then we will soon figure out the length of the longest wormhole in that galaxy which will be calculated by multiplying the radius of the largest black hole by 2. Once done with that we can now equate the sum of the radius of two black holes equal to the length of that wormhole. This equation will help us to know a number of things about the two black holes in connection. We would surely know the radius of one black hole and then form the equation we will be able to find the radius of the other black hole the first one will be connected to. Once we know the radius of both the black holes which are connected we can easily figure out the mass of the two black holes. Once we know the mass of the two black holes we can calculate the evaporation rate of the two black holes and we can easily figure out that till which time the two black hole combination will, convert into a wormhole as we know. Also on the basis of the mass of the two black holes we can calculate the position of the singularity in between them. So now I will brief out the number of things this law provides and I will also explain the working of this law with the help of simple examples of number of black holes known to us. The things explained by this law are:

1.) The radius of the other black hole that may come in combination with the original black hole we are taking as a reference.
2.) The mass of the two black holes that have come together to make a combination.
3.) The evaporation rate of the black hole
4.) The time limit after which the combination of both the black holes will convert into a real wormhole containing a black hole and a white hole.
5.) The position of singularity in between the combination of both the black holes.
6.) The length of the longest wormhole we might want to travel in a particular galaxy.

As we can see that the above information that has been explained by the law is enormous and there are a lot of things which will help us to understand and gain the in depth knowledge regarding the cosmos. The major observation is that more we know about the black holes and their web systems the wormholes the more we will be able to know about the space around our home planet and this will allow us to understand the observable universe around us more and more effectively.

Before discussing the examples of the law I would like to discuss one of the most important things regarding the law, this law establishes a trend within the number of black holes in a galaxy. This trend will be followed by the all the black holes present in a particular galaxy, this means no black hole can turn a face onto this trend and has to follow it under any circumstances.

The trend starts from the smallest black hole in the galaxy, as no black hole has the singularity as it was stated earlier, the smaller black holes which won't be able to rupture the space time will have to make combinations with other black holes making a singularity occur in between them. So therefore to make the longest length possible as per the largest black hole in the galaxy, it has to get connected with a large black hole, The black hole with which this smallest black hole will make the combination will be largest among all the black holes with which the combinations will be made. So let's for simplicity mark the black hole of the galaxy we are talking about to be black hole 1 and the black hole with which it will get connected to be black hole 2. So we interpret that in case 1 the black hole 1 will be the smallest and the black hole 2 will be the largest. As the mass of the black hole 1 will start to increase means we will start taking up black holes heavier than the smallest black hole the size of the black hole 2 will start on decreasing, this means the black hole with which the initial black hole will get connected will become smaller and smaller in order to maintain the length of the largest wormhole a constant as described in law 5. As we will continue on this stage we will come up to the largest black hole in the galaxy and to maintain the constant derived from it the black hole with which it will get connected will be equal to the its own size or the in other words a black hole having a mass equal to the largest black hole in the galaxy will make a connection with the largest black hole in the galaxy. To avoid confusion we can say that when we will reach the largest black hole in the galaxy the mass of the black hole 1 will be equal to the mass of the black hole 2. This trend is really important and will help us to understand the various black holes with which the black holes can get connected. Now it is still natural to ask that won't the trend continue after we reach the position where the size of black hole 1 is equal to the size of the black hole 2? The answer is a big no because as it follows from the laws mentioned, the black hole where this condition will occur it will be the largest black hole of the galaxy, so after that there will be no black hole larger than that and the trend will break down there and will not continue thereafter.

Now we will concentrate on the examples of the galaxies which will also give clarity of the trend mentioned above

For simplicity we will work out the case of the Milky Way galaxy, this is because Milky Way is our home galaxy and it will be very easy for the humanity to study the home galaxy rather than any other galaxy. Therefore if we are now trying to study the Milky Way Galaxy then the largest black hole that we are bound to study is the black hole that lurks at the center of the Milky Way that is none other than the Sagittarius A and now according to the certain laws that I have mentioned above all the black holes in the milky way will be studied with reference to that black hole only.

Now as per trend let's start with the smallest black hole in the Milky Way. The smallest black hole in the Milky Way is XTE J1650-500 and weighs somewhat 4 solar masses. Now the radius of that black hole is 12 km. It is the smallest known black hole that is present in our galaxy. Now as per the laws specified above we know that if the Sagittarius A is the largest black hole in the Milky Way galaxy then the length of the largest wormhole will be about 44 million kilo meter. So let the radius of the second black hole that will be connecting with our main wormhole be x

Now as per the assumptions and the laws which have been proposed the equation will be formed as follows:

The radius of XTE J1650-550 + x = 44 million kilo meter

So therefore the radius of the black hole with which it will be connected will be of radius 43,999,988 km. So now we have completed the first step and found out the radius of the two black holes. The next step is to calculate the mass, the mass of XTE J1650-500 is about 4 solar masses and the mass of the other black hole that will be connected with will have the mass around 14 million solar masses. From the size and the radius it is quite clear that this black hole will be very, large indeed. And this example will also work as a verification of my trend. As being the smallest in the galaxy The XTE black hole will get connected with the largest black hole. Also when we will observe the other black holes in the galaxy we will note that the size of the connecting black hole keeps on decreasing until it will be equal to the mass of the largest black hole in the galaxy that is 4 million solar masses. So therefore we can say that the trend is quite observable because we can easily conclude and say that the mass of the connecting black holes will decrease staring from the largest being the 14 million solar masses and the smallest being the 4 million solar masses. All the other black holes will lie in between this range. Now once we know the radius and the masses of both the black holes we can start up our work of understanding the other things which will help us to know more about the two black holes connected. First of all it is quite easy to calculate the position of the center point (point from where the radius will be calculated of the two). Here there is an important thing to note, as I have mentioned it earlier that the places where the older singularities were believed to be existed will have the centres of the structures of the wormholes containing a black hole and a white hole. Now the converse of the same thing will happen, as we have discussed thing above that the black hole combination like the ones we are explaining above have a singularity somewhere between their total paths. So now that singularity will act as a reference point or the center from where the radius of the two black holes will be connected. This will lead to the formation of a new law that will be explained in a greater detail later. Now once we consider this law we will be able to know the point form where the radius of the two black holes were calculated and we will also be able to know the position of the singularity between the two. According to our point of view, the black hole which will be seen first will be XTE J1650-500 so therefore we can easily estimate that the position will be around 12 kilometer into the tunnel connecting both the black holes. Now once we know the position of the singularity, the radius and the mass of the two black holes combining, we can study deeper and can also find the evaporation rate of the two. The evaporation rate means the time after which a black hole will lose all of its mass to the hawking radiation and will thus disappear. This will be very helpful to us because once we know the time after which one of the black holes in the combination will evaporate we will be able to identify the time after which the combination of the two black holes will soon enough turn out to form a wormhole. Because when a black hole evaporates condition being it is not connected with a white hole all of the energy will burst open into the space and a new doorway will open into the web of the space time, allowing more and more matter to go in between the different universes. A solar mass black hole will take about 10^{64} years to evaporate. So if we look for the smaller side the XTE J1650-500 black hole weighing about 4 solar mass will take about $4*10^{64}$ years to evaporate, thus it will take a very long time for it to evaporate. This time is greater than the age of the universe too. So I think this will not be a good step to know the evaporation time for the system to be a wormhole.

Let's suppose the condition where XTE J1650-500 evaporates just in a fraction of seconds. If this happens what will happen. The events that will be recorded by the humanity are as follows:

1.) A bright light will appear in the sky because this black hole (XTE J1650-500) is present in the Milky Way galaxy.
2.) We will observe very high amount of energy getting released from the system. This energy is nothing else but all the matter that was present in the singularity in our galaxy. But here is the moment where some peculiar tricks will happen.
3.) Now when we will observe the system very closely or somehow the black hole on the other side we will find that the mass of the black hole on other side will get a little bit lower than before and therefore its size will also decrease.
4.) Now if the size of the black hole decreases along with its mass it is quite clear that the radius of the black hole will also decrease.

After this list of observations a question might occur in our mind that what is the reason behind the radius of the black hole decreasing on the other side? This is some very strange event that can occur. Also the reason might not come in the form that Hawking Radiation was the reason of such a decrease in the radius of the black hole. We know that Hawking radiation apply up to a negligible state to any black hole which has a mass in thousands of solar masses. But the black hole that we are currently talking about here has the mass 14 million solar masses it is even bigger than the Sagittarius A, so therefore it is very unnatural to happen. Now as an application we can figure out and see that when the singularity broke down with the evaporation of XTE J1650-500, a lot of mass exited the structure. Now according to the laws mentioned above when a wormhole forms with a black hole and a white hole at the either ends of the center point, the point from which the radius of the black holes would have been measured has to lie at the center of the structure named wormhole. Means that distance of the white hole and the black hole must be equal from that point. Now here in order to make that point possible the other black hole that was having a mass of 14 million solar masses has to reduce its radius, as a result of which the center point will come to be associated really at the center of the wormhole structure. This is very important paragraph as it explains the post evaporation events of a black hole and will explain that if a black hole is connected with another black hole what will happen if one of them completely dies. Now it will be very interesting here to understand one more thing and thing will explain what will happen if a black hole is connected with a white hole. As we don't have much information about the white hole the only thing about which we can predict is the black hole itself. Now when a black hole will be connected with a white hole, it is natural that they have to maintain the distance in between them in such a way that the center point remains at the center of the structure totally. Now in order to do that if the black hole evaporates a little bit the white hole has to make sure and reduce its radius up to the level till which it has its radius equal to the little bit evaporated black hole radius. Let's consider for the simplicity a black hole of radius 4 million kilometer then the radius of wormhole will be 4 million kilometers too. Let's consider that the black hole evaporates its size and the radius becomes 3 million kilometer. So for this the radius of white hole will too has to become 3 million kilometer. The radius of the white hole here refers to its distance from the center point. Once both the radius becomes 3 million kilometer the center point will again be at the center. Now suppose the evaporation of the black hole carries on. As the evaporation of the black hole will continue so will the reduction of the radius of the white hole and once this happens there will be a point when both the white hole and the black hole has to coincide. Now what happens if the two points of a straight line coincides with each other, either the line forms a circle or it becomes of length zero. The case we take up here is that the length becomes zero because we are type of stretching the black hole and white hole towards the center point of the structure and once both of them reach at the center point the length reduces to become zero and once that happens the doorway in between the two universes will completely disappear until the time a new black hole is not formed. So above are the two cases where I have described the outcomes of a black hole evaporating one where it was connected with another black hole and one where it was connected with a white hole. This step till now is the indication of the application of all the five laws up to the Law 5. Here I have described certain question which may occur once we study the laws and secondly I have also addressed the question of how can we consider that the wormhole closes if the black hole evaporates completely?

With this let's continue and try to understand Law 6, the Law 7 and finally the Law 8

Law 6) This law states that out of the total number of combinations that will be made by a black hole 50% of them will be with white holes and 50% of them will be black holes. This means that for example if a black hole makes two combinations one of them will be with a white hole and one of them will be with black hole. This is because both of them are somewhat identical only the difference in them is on the basis of their some properties like one sucks the things and the other releases the things out. They mostly have the same properties despite the above difference that have been mentioned.

Law 7) This law explains how the position of singularity which will change between the various structures as we consider the black holes present in a particular Galaxy. This law will help us to identify that at which limit the singularity may present in the structure of combination of two black holes and will be very helpful in deciding the mass of the second black hole in the combination without using any of the laws above and once we know that as explained we can find a lot of things about the system easily. So this Law will also be based upon the trend of the black hole combinations as it is followed in a particular galaxy. We have studied and understood that the smallest black hole in the galaxy will be connected with the largest black hole. I also explained it with the help of an example that is given above. So in that case we found that the singularity will be present at the lowest distance in comparison to the other black hole combinations. Here we must understand that higher the mass of the second black hole the nearer the singularity will be present to the first black hole. Here the second black hole refers to the black hole with which the connection is made and the first black hole refers to the black hole in the galaxy which is making the connection. With the help of the trend we noted we also know that as the mass of the first black hole will rise means that we started to take more and more massive black holes in the galaxy then the mass of the second black hole will start to decrease and thus the singularity will start to shift on the other end, now we also know the maximum limit of the mass of black hole in a galaxy is the mass of the most massive black hole in the galaxy after that the mass of the black hole will not increase as till then we would have reached the maximum limit of the mass of the black hole, once we reach that limit then the singularity will reach the middle part of the whole structure because the mass on both the end will be even due to the laws given above and as a result the trend in the singularity will be shifting from the extreme left to the middle as we keep on increasing the mass of the black hole we are taking in the reference galaxy.

Now a question that arises is that how will it be possible for us to decide the mass of the other black hole just on the basis of examining the position of singularity? The answer to this part is quite simple.

Suppose we enter the smallest black hole in the Milky way, sure enough it will be connected with the largest black hole, now here supposing that we don't really know the trend the only thing that we know is that the largest black hole with which the Milky Way can connect (means the smallest black hole in the milky way can connect) is 14 million solar masses and the smallest being 4 million solar masses, then on seeing the position of the singularity which will be located at extreme left we can say that singularity being on the extreme left would mean that the connecting black hole is the most massive because if we go in any other black hole massive that the earlier one the singularity will be shifted we can guess the mass of the connecting black hole and that will come to be as 14 million solar masses.

I know that is a little bit tricky to understand so in order to remove any kind of question or confusion that may occur in the mind of scientists, I am now giving a detailed set of Diagrams which will show how the mass of the black holes on the either ends of the structure will affect the position of singularity within the structure. The images are given below

Image 1:

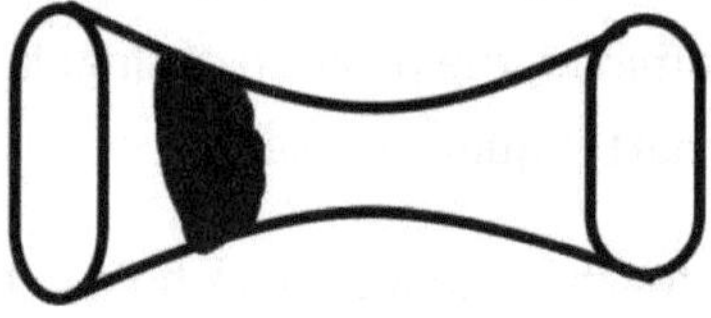

Here we can note that the singularity is on the left most corner of the structure, the ends of the structure have been labelled as Black hole 1 and black hole 2, now as the singularity is on the left hand side we can easily comprehend that black hole 2 is more massive than the black hole 1, the reason behind such an assumption is because more massive the black hole more will be its size and more will be the size of black hole the more matter will it engulf at a particular time and the less mass the black hole the less matter will it engulf, thus the amount of matter entering the structure will be more from the right hand side than the left hand side, due to this all matter which was about to settle in between the structure will shift to the left hand side as more force is laid on the accumulated matter by the Right hand side not by the left hand and therefore by seeing the position of singularity as so we can easily comprehend that black hole 1 is smaller than black hole 2. Now here as per the given conditions we can easily say that black hole one is smallest black hole because we chose it to be so and therefore black hole 2 will be the largest black hole which will get connected. Now as black hole one is the smallest black hole we can easily say that the singularity will not shift more on the left hand side but will now start to shift on the right hand side and will reach a certain limit after which it can't really shift more on the right hand side and that will be the trend of the singularity which will be followed up by different black holes in the galaxy. Also some more images have been added below to make this trend easier to understand.

Image 2:

As we can see above, this image has four scenarios, at all the four scenarios the singularity is at different locations. A thing which is worth noting is that after the fourth scenario the singularity is not shifting on the right hand side and that scenario is the place which is the limit for the singularity to move in a particular galaxy. Although in each galaxy the fourth scenario may be present at different locations but where ever it is present it will label the limit beyond which the singularity can't move. Now let's try to understand each and every scenario which has been labelled in the image and search for an effective answer which will indicate that how these scenarios are achieved and in which combinations we can see the scenarios like above, although it is quite clear that wherever the singularity is present on the other side will always have a black hole which may be massive or equal in size to the black hole which we can see from the Earth.

Scenario 1: This scenario has the singularity a little bit shifted on the right hand side in reference to the position of singularity in the image 1. Thus because the singularity has shifted a little bit on the Right hand side we can say that the black hole 1 which we are seeing or entering is not the smallest black hole but a black hole which a little bit massive than the smallest black hole, thus we can also say that the black hole will now start on reducing its size and is little bit smaller than the largest black hole 2 as we noted in the image 1, thus here we can note that as the singularity keeps on ascending to the right hand side the size of the black hole 1 increases and the size of the black hole 2 decreases, it is important to note that the increase and the decrease in the size of the black hole and the black hole 2 respectively will be up to a certain limit which will be described in the scenario 4

Scenario 2 and scenario 3: Now again the same trend follows and as the singularity keeps on moving towards the right side the size of black hole 1 keeps on increasing whereas the size of the black hole 2 keeps on decreasing. These scenarios are just located in between the special scenarios of the singularity on the extreme left as in image 1 and the singularity reaching its limit which will be described in the next scenario.

Scenario 4: Now here at this point we will likely reach the largest black hole in the galaxy and according to all the laws given above the black hole 1 and black hole 2 will have to be of the same size in order to compensate the total distance in between the two ends which has to be equal to the longest wormhole which will be formed in the galaxy. Now at this point the singularity will acquire the center most position in between the structure, the main reason behind it is that the rate of particles entering the structure will be same from both the sides and thus equal force will be generated upon the singularity from both the ends and because of that the singularity will neither move on the left hand side nor on the right hand side and thus it will remain concentrated at the center and once one of the black hole evaporates they will form the longest wormhole in the galaxy. So thus it is quite clear that once we reach to the scenario 4 we will be observing the largest black hole in the galaxy on both the ends of the structure and the singularity will ultimately stop its process of shifting here and there in the structure and will come to a halt until one of the black hole evaporates perishing the singularity once and for all.

So this is the end of law 7 which describes about the various positions of singularity which may occur between the different combinations of black holes.

Law 8) This Law tells us that at a time how many combinations are there which a black hole can make. This is very important as then we can know that how many universes are there? Before explaining this thing that how can we know the number of universes are there, I must first state the Law that describes to make this important discovery and explain the implication regarding it.

The law states that the number of combination that a black hole can make at a particular time will be equal to 2 times the radius of the black hole. The radius of the black hole is located after the innermost stable orbit; it is the region where the photons orbit the black holes. It (Innermost stable orbit) is the only layer which is also known by the name Photon Sphere and is the last region where objects are known to orbit the black hole easily. After this the layer or the region which comes up is the black hole itself starting from its event horizon. This also indicates the starting of the main region of the black hole. And crossing it means that you are going to enter the black hole any time soon. So with respect to the indication of the black hole this layer is very significant. With this significance now this layer has another role to play which will be very helpful for the humanity that is to help us know the final layer where the photons can stay in a good position but after that a simple kick to the photons would mean that they would enter the black hole and will never be ever seen by this galaxy. Once we know the number of combination a black holes make we will be able to know various things about it.

First of let's know that how can we calculate the innermost stable orbit of any black hole. It is basically calculated with the help of the radius of the black hole.

It is located at a distance three times the distance of the radius of the black hole. So now in order to find the number of combinations that a black hole will make we have to just multiply the radius by 2. Let's take the example again of the nearest super massive black holes that is the Sagittarius A. The radius of the Sagittarius A is 22 million kilometers thus it is evident that the number of combination that the Sagittarius A will make will be equal to 44 million combinations. These combinations will include both the black holes and the white hole. Now as the properties of the black holes and the white holes are quite same just despite the fact that one sucks in the objects and the other one release the objects out. So we can say that 50% of these combinations will be with black holes and the other 50% will account for the combinations to be made with white holes as described above. This means out of 44 million combinations 22 million will be with black holes and the other 22 million combinations will be with white holes. Now here we will get another proof regarding the existence of multiple universes or the parallel universes. Although if I am considering the concept of the existence of the wormholes in the research, it is quite evident, that I am considering the theory of existence of multiple universes to be true. But here the main point about which I am talking about is the parallel universes. The universes which are the same as our universe only the problem with them is that they can be set in past or in future. For the proof to make sense it is important that we must follow the trend that has been labelled in the above laws because in the absence of the knowledge of that trend it will be very difficult to understand the black hole combinations. If we are taking the Sagittarius A into account the galaxy we have to consider is the Milky Way and it has been stated above that the length of the longest wormhole that will be formed in the Milky Way will be of the length 44 million kilometres. Now if Sagittarius A makes out 44 million combinations and 22 million out of them are with black holes, then the radius of the black holes it will make combinations with will be about 22 million too, this is because the Sagittarius A is the largest black hole in the Milky way and it will follow up the case where the radius of both the black holes connecting will be equal to each other and this case will be followed according to the trend too. Now this means that the 22 million black holes will have a mass of about 4 million solar masses and radius 22 million kilometres. And in astrophysics if we take two black holes and find that they have the same mass and the same radius then we consider the black holes to be identical or same. This means that if Sagittarius A makes the combinations with the black holes that are of the mass and the radius that is the same as of the Sagittarius A, this means it is making combinations with itself. Here we can't just say and conclude that this means that there is no wormhole as a black hole is making combination with itself. But according to the exotic matter theory if the gate is open then a wormhole is open and if a black hole is making combinations with the other white holes it is making combination with black holes too, because if we say that there are no black holes with which the combination will be made it means that there will be no white holes with which the combinations will be made as we have stated that the number of combinations with white holes will be the same with the number of combination with the black holes, thus assuming that there will be no black hole at the other end will be the same as stating that there is no white hole at the other end but this can't be the scenario as the doorway or the black hole is wide open. But now another question arises that if there is a singularity in between then there must be no tachyons passing through, and then the combinations of the black holes must not exist? Yeah this is a correct question to be thought of but the answer to this question is quite simple, if we consider the Tachyons to be passing through the doorways very effectively then they must have the ability to manipulate their speed and just to say that their speed is more than the speed of light is wrong. The reason for me here to consider that the Tachyons have the ability to manipulate speeds is because they travel through a number of black holes and thus they must travel at different speeds in different black holes as the speed to move through each black hole is different and with such high speeds they would easily outsmart the black holes and will be escape the gravity of both the black holes and will in the end not end up in the singularity as they will reach the point long before any matter would be able to make the singularity and under this scenario they will keep circulating through the combination of the black hole keeping it wide open. Now a new question arises after settling the first question. The question is that what will be the effect on the Tachyons once the singularity has been created in between the combination of the two black holes. For the correct answer we have to reconsider the concept of singularity in between the two black holes again. Now as I have explained above once two black holes will combine the matter they will suck, will start to concentrate at any point in between the black holes. Now as the mass of the concentrated matter starts to increase the mass will reach such a stage that the mass will be sufficient to make tiny black holes in between, these tiny black holes will follow up their time period as per the Hawking radiation and will evaporate in some time but the black holes will keep on being made and getting evaporated continuously inside the system, so this will allow space for the tachyons to constantly pass through and the system as described will keep functioning until one of them evaporates. So coming back to the proof of the parallel universe we can say that if Sagittarius A makes a combination with itself this means that there are a lot many universes in which the Sagittarius A is present and the number of such universes is about 22 million, so we can say that there are at least 22 million parallel universes which are containing black holes identical to Sagittarius A. This means that the parallel universes are present and the theory about the existence of such universes is true.

Now to avoid any kind of confusion that may occur regarding the laws, I am stating the laws again with only there statements but not the explanations, also the names of these laws will be explained in this section to give a separate identity to the laws and also to make it quite easy to refer the laws to anyone without giving the statements time and again but just telling the names of the laws.

Law 1: This law states that all the black holes in the Milky Way will be studied in the reference of the Sagittarius A.This law will be known as the **Law of Reference.**

Law 2: This law tells that the points where the older singularities were existing will be present the new center points of the wormhole structures between the black holes and the white holesThis law will be known as the **Law of center points.**

Law 3: This law states that there will be limit on the maximum penetration of the space time in a galaxy which will be decided on the basis of the largest black hole in the galaxy and the space time in that galaxy won't be penetrated beyond that. This law will be known as the **Law of maximum penetration.**

Law 4: This law states that the distance of the white hole and black hole which are connected with each other will be equal from the point of center where the older singularity was thought to exist.

This law will be known as the **Law of the distance from the center of the wormhole.**

Law 5: This law states that when the two black holes may connect to from a singularity at any position in between the structure of the combination of the two black holes the sum of the radius of the two black holes will be equal to the longest worm hole in the galaxy. Also the radius of the two black holes will now be measured from the temporary singularity itself.

This law will be known as the **Law of the sum of radius.**

Law 6: This Law states that out of the total combinations that will be made by a black hole 50% of them will be with the white holes and the 50% of them will be with black holes. So therefore half combinations will be with white holes and half the combination will be made with the black holes. This law is only applicable to the super massive black holes which apply a lot of force on the space time region and therefore penetrate it successfully.

This law will be known as the **Law of 50% combination.**

Law 7: This law states that the singularities in between the black hole combinations will shift following a particular trend and will show at the left most side and in the middle and will be also present in between these two situation.

This law will be known as the **Law of motion of singularity.**

Law 8: This laws states that the total number of combination that will be made by a black hole will be equal to 2 times the radius of the black hole.

This law will be known as the **Law of Black hole Combination.**

Now after listing these laws we are well equipped with the material needed to get the solutions to those obstacles which I had listed before in the chapter 2.

Lets first review those obstacles and then we will try to look out for a solution to those.

So the obstacles were:

1.) How gather such a large mass
2.) The wormhole may open into our original universe but we won't be able to find the path back home
3.) The process of formation may go wrong

Now let's start picking up the solutions one by one:

1.) Yes indeed it is a major problem on how to gather such a large mass which will be needed to make the black hole, but this problem can be effectively solved.
Now to solve this we take up a simple scenario under which we have all the technology and the resources to go at a particular place in the space to create the first ever wormhole of our own, the only problem that has been left to be addressed is the matter that has to be gathered. Now as a solution to this the region where we will target to create the wormhole will of course contain planets, space debris, small satellites and many more so they can be disintegrated and can be used as the matter resource hereby solving the problem completely.

2.) The next problem can be easily be solved with the help of the 8 laws stated above, with the help of these laws we can easily determine that which combination of the black hole will take us to which time period easily by the help of unitary method and further once this is known the travelling through the black hole will be a lot easier than ever.

3.) Now this problem is completely experimental and can't be really given a solution mathematically or theoretically but involves constant experimentation so that we may not fail while creating the exact wormhole on our own.

With this now let's move on to further chapters.

Chapter 4

The new theorem of singularity

In the previous chapter while stating the different laws of black hole combination a term named singularity was stated many times. Now many of you might be wondering what singularity is and why do we need a new theorem pertaining to it. Let me explain in brief but an effective way.

Now as we have already discussed it earlier the wormholes have a deep connection with black holes as when the black holes combine with the white holes what we get is a wormhole. Now the term black hole was defined first time by John Wheeler back in 1960's but the presence of black holes as a definition of gravitational collapsed objects was quoted the first time in the General Theory of Gravity given by Sir Albert

Einstein back in 1915. Now along with the logic of black holes a special term that is singularity was quoted, it in literal meant the end of space and it was thought that all of the matter of black hole was concentrated at this point and it was inescapable, but with the creation of powerful technologies such as small wormholes it is quite evident that the singularity may exist but isn't always at the end of each black hole so therefore a new theory is needed for the understanding of the singularity which has been presented below:

This new theorem of singularity is indeed very important in describing the maze wormhole and the blind folded wormhole, so I considered explaining it first then describing the two wormholes. Now as we know that there are no ends to the space after the black hole since they are connected to the white holes so in this scenario a question arises that can the singularity exist in the real life, the answer comes out be a yes. Now the black hole can't always be connected to the white hole but at times it may get connected to an another black hole. When two black holes get connected the matter that is sucked in by both of them get accumulated at the centre as the result of which a temporary singularity is formed, why is it temporary? The answer is that when lot of matter will get accumulated at the centre the mass will go so high that it can create small tiny black holes within the two major black holes. Now as each and every black holes follows up the Hawking radiation and the smaller ones show it at a higher rate, then it is obvious that these tiny black holes that have formed using the mass of the temporary singularity will evaporate and once they get evaporated they will form up space for the new black holes to form continuing the process till both of them are working. But when one of them will get evaporated it will open up as a white hole which will connect with the second black hole and thus will form a normal system of the wormhole. This should be considered that the black hole – black hole system won't sustain for long in comparison to the normal wormhole systems. But it must be noted that Tachyons will pass through the black hole-black hole combinations in a way which will be described later. To make the concept of the black hole singularity more easy to understand I am adding the following image in the research paper.

This image will be explained so that no confusion is left in mind of the readers after reading this new concept of singularity.

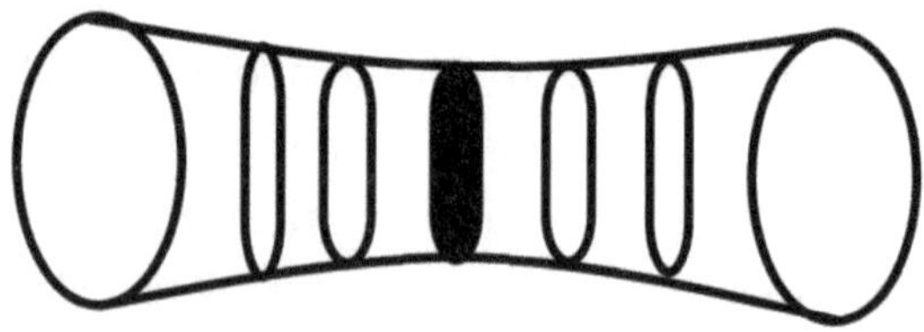

Now here we can see that at the center is the singularity which is darkened in between the structure of the Black hole 1 and Black hole 2. The singularity is darkened in between and as explained above it is temporary in nature. Here to avoid confusion I have only marked four black holes but in actual case there will be black hole present at every inch within the structure, and closer the black hole is to the singularity the smaller it is and it will show the hawking radiation at a much faster rate than the other black holes. The smallest black holes will be present nearest to the singularity.

Now with the introduction of new theorem of singularity I would like to put forward two new kinds of wormholes which will be present or may be formed as a consequence of the theorem.

The two new kinds of wormholes are the maze wormhole and the blind fold wormhole as listed below:

These are two special types of wormholes that are introduced in the research. There is a physical limit on how many white holes may get connected to a black hole. Such a black hole will have a number of paths connecting to different parts of the universes so the resulting figure inside the black hole will be like a maze so it will be known as the maze wormhole. Now there is nothing to prevent the black hole to even get connected to other black holes when this happens some of the path will be closed due to the formation of the singularity while some of the paths will be open due to the connection with white holes as a result they will be known as the blinded folded wormholes with some of the paths open and some closed. Mostly the probability to find the blind fold wormhole will be more than the probability to find the maze wormhole. This is because ideally a black hole will be connected both with the white holes and the other black holes at the same time but finding a black hole that is only connected with only the white holes will be quite difficult, so mostly the kind of wormholes that will be found will be the blind fold wormholes

Chapter 5

The procedure

Now if we are discussing a formula we also must know how to apply it so that no stone is left unturned in studying of the formula.

So the procedure of this has been explained below:

The basic concept that will be used to create a wormhole is to force down a lot of mass in the space time region so that the space time begins to bend but as we know that as each black hole do not becomes a part of the wormhole the main reason being that it is not having enough mass that the space time region bends to such an extent that it tears apart opening on the other end in the form of a white hole, so we must put the mass of a super massive in the place of in the formula so that the resulting mass is so large that it tears up the space apart. Once it is done our black hole will be formed and because of being a super massive black hole it will be a part of the resulting wormhole which will connect to our universe making a way back home.

Now the last thing that has been left to discuss in the formula is if experimentally this formula can be tested and the answer is a big yes. Now a question arises how can this be done, now to do this a simple experiment has already been performed where a wormhole has been created in the lab now we can calculate the mass needed to make that wormhole and if it numerically matches with the mass that has already been used then it is quite obvious that our formula is correct

Now along with let's consider one more fact that is time travel

We know that time travel is one of the most amusing things in the vast topics covered in the field of space and cosmos, many have tried to theorize this concept but still the humanity is not able to reach to nay conclusion regarding this, but this theorem that has been presented in the book may provide a solution to this

Now in the 8 applications of black hole formations we saw an amusing fact, the fact was that the black holes make the combinations with white holes and which will be equal to the radius of the black hole,

Now we know that the big bang occurred 13.8 billion years ago, so we can divide the time period of each universe by diving the age of the universe with the number of combinations the black hole is making with the white hole.

As an example, let's consider Sag A, it radius is 2,19,19,023km thus it will make these much combinations with the white holes and on doing division we get 62.95901053619041 thus the difference between two combinations will be almost 63 years so if combination A takes us 5 million years back combination B just after A will take us 5million -63 years back making a simple Arithmetic progression

With this lets move onto the final chapter that is the conclusion

Chapter 6

Conclusion

Now it is the time to end this book which concentrated on the formula to make man made wormholes. Along with this the book also provided the 8 laws of black hole combination which will make us better understand the way the black hole combines and once we are through with all of this the book provides us with the presence of two new kind of wormholes and the new theorem of singularities. In all with the help of this book I have tries to cover some of the unsolved mysteries of the wormholes and have tries to fill in the knowledge gaps with my new theories.

With this part completed the more upcoming books will put light on formulas that I have discovered for time travel, a new kind of machine, how to create the space ship which will help us to move through wormholes.

So with this I finally conclude this part of the series see you all !!

Printed by Libri Plureos GmbH in Hamburg,
Germany